S0-BCR-358

Boldrini

LEARN THE VALUE OF

Trust

◆

by ELAINE P. GOLEY

Illustrated by Debbie Crocker

◆

ROURKE ENTERPRISES, INC.
VERO BEACH, FL 32964

Britannica Home Library Service, Inc. offers a
varied selection of bookcases. For details on
ordering, please write:

Britannica Home Library Service, Inc.
310 South Michigan Avenue
Chicago, Illinois 60604
Attn: Customer Service

© 1987 Rourke Enterprises, Inc.

All rights reserved. No part of this book may be
reproduced or utilized in any form or by any
means, electronic or mechanical including
photocopying, recording or by any information
storage and retrieval system without permission in
writing from the publisher.

Library of Congress Cataloging-in-Publication Data

Goley, Elaine P., 1949–
  Learn the value of trust.

  Summary: Depicts situations that demonstrate the
meaning and importance of trust.
    1. Trust (Psychology)—Juvenile literature.
[1. Trust (Psychology)   2. Conduct of life]
I. Title.   II. Title: Trust.
BF575.T7G65   1987   158'.2   87-16319
ISBN 0-86592-378-7

Trust

Do you know what **trust** is?

Trust is letting Sam borrow your favorite book because you know he'll take care of it.

You're **trusting** because you know Tom's dog won't
bite you if you're gentle with him.

Trust is knowing that a visit to the doctor will help you stay well, even if it hurts a little.

Your teacher **trusts** you not to look at someone else's paper when you take a test.

When John tells you a secret he **trusts** you not
to tell anyone.

Your cat **trusts** you to be gentle when you play with her.

Your parents **trust** you to tell them where you're
going to play because they want you to be safe.

You **trust** your dad to tell you the truth when you ask him a question.

Your dog **trusts** you to feed him every day.

Knowing that your mom and dad will come back for
you when they leave you with the babysitter is **trust.**

When you promise to help Cynthia with her book report, she **trusts** you to keep your word.

You **trust** your friend Terry to take care of your bike when he rides it.

Your parents **trust** you to come right home after school.

When you hold your little brother, he **trusts** you
not to let him fall.

Your dad **trusts** you to talk with him when you have a problem.

Trust is knowing that your parents love you,
even when you break a window.

Trust is knowing you can depend on someone.

Trust

"It's so hot. A good day to sell lemonade," said Carlos.

He and his mother made two pitchers of lemonade. Then Carlos brought them outside.

"I'd like a glass of lemonade," said Mrs. Smith. She handed Carlos 10 cents.

Rita and Van rode up to the stand on their bikes. They bought two glasses of lemonade. After Rita and Van left, Tony walked by. Carlos and Tony were good friends.

"Carlos, Grandma is on the phone," yelled his mother from the kitchen window.

"Tony, will you watch my stand awhile?" asked Carlos as he ran into the house.

"Sure," answered Tony.

A few minutes later, Carlos came back to his stand. Tony was gone.

"What happened to my lemonade? And where's my money?" said Carlos.

How did Carlos show he **trusted** Tony?
How do you show you **trust** your friends?

Trust

The children were excited. Today the class was going to Mr. Brown's farm.

"Remember," said their teacher, Mrs. Lowe, "you must stay with your group. And Mr. Brown doesn't want you to pet the animals."

The children piled onto the bus. They sang songs all the way to the farm.

"Look at the horse," said Mel as he got off the bus.

"Those piglets are so hungry," said Alice.

"I'm going to feed that big goose some of my crackers," said Fred.

"Don't!" yelled Brenda.

"Ouch! It bit my finger," yelled Fred.

Mrs. Lowe ran over to Fred. She looked at his finger.

"We'll have to get you to a doctor," she said. "Sorry, class, the field trip is over."

How did Fred show he couldn't be **trusted?**

How do you show your teacher that you can be **trusted?**